Letters to Buddha

Victor M. Depta

Blair Mountain Press
114 East Campbell Street
Frankfort, Kentucky 40601

Blair Mountain Press
114 East Campbell Street
Frankfort, Kentucky 40601

Publisher's Cataloging-in-Publication

Depta, Victor.
    [Poems. Selections]
    Letters to Buddha / Victor M. Depta.
    pages cm
    LCCN 2015939652
    ISBN 978-0-9768817-9-7

    1. Enlightenment (Buddhism)--Poetry. I. Title.

PS3554.E64A6 2015   811'.54
                      QBI15-600121

Cover art by the author. The photograph on the back cover—of the *I Love Mountains Day*, Frankfort, Kentucky, February 12, 2015—is courtesy of the author.

http://www.blairmtp.net

CONTENTS

Winter

Spring

Postscript: History and Fate

Foreword: The Noumena

My daughter, as she was proofreading these poems, said to me several times that I should write a brief introduction to them because I was presenting a difficult subject and using terminology the reader might not be familiar with. After giving her suggestion some thought, I decided to write a short essay on my understanding of enlightenment and the four qualities of human mentation.

The experience of enlightenment has been recorded so many times that it has become a fact of life, yet the results of it, and its interpretations, are so varied and irrational as to make the subject questionable and oftentimes fraudulent. A human being has a pre-rational experience of unity with the phenomenal world, during which he or she feels liberated from the constraints of ordinary existence, feelings which might include fearful awe but more often are of ecstasy and joy. Since the experience is pre-rational, nothing can be said about it other than reporting on the emotional response, although a multitude of religious and metaphysical interpellations have been added to the experience over the centuries.

I assume that what happened to me at the age of thirty was an experience of enlightenment, and I immediately set about explaining, or attempting to explain, what it meant. Because my literary interests lay in the 19th Century with the Romantics and the Transcendentalists, I assumed that my unity was with a benign presence imbuing phenomena. Later, in a slightly more sophisticated manner, I conjectured that unity was with the Kantian noumenon, that reality of a phenomenon beyond the five senses, the noumenal *thing-in-itself* which is an unexperienceable mystery. Much later I realized that my trans-phenomenal interpretation of enlightenment, both the romantic and the metaphysical, were futile efforts at forcing an artificial design— the symbolic world of humanity—onto the non-symbolic world of phenomena.

However, since I believed that my enlightenment was with something rather than a self-referential excitation—that noumenal reality was experienceable, albeit ineffable—I used it in the creation of a rational philosophy of mysticism. Noumenal reality became the substance of phenomena with the caveat that it had no rational meaning. It was the ontological meaningless meaning of existence. Satisfied with my interpretation of Kantian noumena, I went on to create a hierarchy of our mental states: the Self, Consciousness, Self-Consciousness, and Pure Consciousness (I had earlier included the Ego as part of the hierarchy, but realizing that the Freudian id and ego are incorporated in the Self, I dropped that idea). The Self is what any animal is in its existence (I would include plants), with particular emphasis on its unity with all other animals and plants on the earth, all as having their own existential ontology. The other three are not entities but processes, activities and functions of the Self. Consciousness is the Self in any intentional state, intuited or spoken. Self-Consciousness is the ability to objectify the Self as a third-person entity, he or she, in any dramatic situation wherein the isolated subjectivity of the Self is in an objective relationship with others, whether they be other people or phenomena. And since Self-Consciousness is utterly dependent on the symbolic constructs of language, it does not have an existential ontology. It is an epiphenomenon of language and is thus twice removed from phenomenal reality. Self-Consciousness is the result of language, and language—its symbolic essence—is separated from non-symbolic phenomena. Pure Consciousness is the ability to forgo the intentional concerns of the Self, of Conscious intent, and of the rationalizations of Self-Consciousness. In its freedom, it can experience enlightenment, which I had assumed was union with something, with noumenal reality, which I considered a rational term for *nirvana* in Buddhism.

So, I equated Self-Consciousness, once removed from Pure Consciousness, as an epiphenomenon of language and a synonym for *annata*, the Buddhist no-self, which left the Self (and its Consciousness)—however liable to change, suffering and death—as ontological realities in the phenomenal world. The liberation from Self-Consciousness was a joy of nothingness: noumenal reality is a meaningless meaning and phenomenal reality does not recognize our language world. Nothingness might lead to the despair of a Schopenhauer or a Nietzsche (or Ayn Rand and rampant, predatory capitalism), but it can also lead to the realization that suffering is universal and that life cries out for succor and deliverance. Out of that realization rises compassion; out of it rises Christ, Buddha, and a conviction of the world's holiness.

My beautiful Buddha, the one who desired the end of suffering, he was now philosophically suspect, and what a fool I had been, deluding myself into thinking of him as the incarnate, compassionate one, when he was, rather, attempting to overcome change and death by denying the significance of the self and the material world which sustains it. The poems, my *Letters to Buddha*, support the opposite: the self and the material world are the source and substance of all reality. There is no escaping from it, not even through enlightenment with its ecstasy of eternity.

As I was writing the poems in this volume, there was an insistent pain and sorrowing in the tone of many of them, until I came to a final realization. My vaunted noumenal reality was either a philosophical construction, a mere metaphysics of rational understanding which has nothing to do with the experience of enlightenment, or it was an existent reality which I experienced during enlightenment, a union of myself with the source of all phenomena. But there can be an ultimate realization. Noumenal reality needn't be trans-phenomenal. It is phenomena experienced without a language context, related in a way to Spinoza's unity of the individual and nature, reality at one time an "attribute of thought" and at another time an "attribute of extension." *Noumenal reality and phenomenal reality are one. Samsara and nirvana are one.* For an elaboration of these ideas, the reader might want to follow them in my two books of essays on the subject.* In any case, our liberation (as well as the knowledge that enlightenment—the freedom from the constraints of epiphenomenal Self-Consciousness and language) is justification itself for joy and ecstasy without the need for anything trans-phenomenal, whether it be a noumenal reality, a Christ's resurrection, or a Buddhist's *nirvana*. In the purity of nothingness, we are free to love, to be loving-kind and compassionate.

The Simultaneous Mountain: Essays and Poetry on Mysticism
Blair Mountain Press 2005 ISBN 0-9768817-0-5

Twofold Consciousness: Poetry and Essays on Mysticism
Blair Mountain Press 2012 ISBN 978-0-9768817-7-3

Summer

July
ah, sweat in the eyes
again

The Cow Path

a metaphysics that would
out of the stone-well of the Self
where the earth seeps and sweetens Consciousness
define what they are

or find a happiness on the eyes
merely, and hear what fragrance
oh, and touch stippled pears and plums
and melons, thoughtlessly

it would explain
lo, they're but a flow of emptiness
only convenient words, and Self-Consciousness too
for an identity elsewhere, not in the *skandhas*

and the somethings in addition to phenomena
beyond the senses, what the mind can never know
these Kantian exemptions we presume as real
those mysterious noumena

although on a ridge
following an old cow path to my great uncle's
pausing for a while among the sumac, the thistles and greenbriers
the sapling poplars and the scrub sourwoods

there was, for a moment
no longer any need of explaining
not of the mountains, or clouds or sky
or any begotten of sunlight, or birthed of the mind
this not to be and Being
this other ecstasy and light
and all delight

The Canticle

> *brother sun, sister moon*
> Saint Francis of Assisi

to let ourselves go in bliss
the sweet Self and its Pure-Conscious ecstasy
but always the stay, the cynic of Self-Consciousness
as if joy were a none-such, a mystic troubadour among physics

but why not a desire that lingers in Self-Consciousness
as the moon does
though it passes, bedecked with clouds and stars
and though we merely glimpse, through the trees
the pale gold, it lingers as a paradigm
and suffuses the mind

or as the sun does
flamingo-feathered at dawn, that loveliness we long for
desirous as the leaves which devour the light—
and its rouged, subtle glory at twilight
although it fades, pervades us as a paradigm
as an image, and lingers as a voice
a rune, a manna
when bliss is the sun and moon

A Lullaby

if it were true
as the ancient Aryans wrote in the *Vedas*
that words create reality
that to name is to realize out of the void
say, a hummingbird we could gaze at
briefly, as it sips from a trumpet blossom
and the words *slender* and *curved* and *beak*
and *scarlet* and *orange*
appear

and the first Adam naming the creatures in his Eden
and the other as the Logos of the world—
if all that were true
would every utterance, then, create reality anew
even the gossipy banal, the newscasters' clichés
the political bromides, the sports chatter
the ceremonial repetition of those who kneel
in gratitude and deliverance

or a lullaby
momma's going to buy you a mocking bird—
in the child's mind
would it have wings
brown wings, and in flight, white feathers
and as a boy or girl
hearing for the first time its variable trill
what we call beautiful, and holy
would they create, anew
their voices rising
a name for paradise

Magnolia Seeds

the blossoms, among their sprays of leaves
are uncountable
white, pungent, almost vulgar—
why would one choose them
in their green panoply
as a resemblance to
—brazenly coy, and scented—
what Enlightenment is

since the metaphor is tediously ancient
older than the cross
that barren tree on which redemption hangs
that haggard blossom of flesh
delivering to the sky its seedless eternity

why choose the fragrant, white presences
not immemorial as the sea and sky
or infinite as the galaxies
why choose suffering, the petals shriveling, falling
the grotesque pods of seeds, their myriad waste
but for the wistful, redolent light they were
their ecstasy in all that haste

Apples and Pears

in the simplicity of my thought
Brahman and *atman* are baffling words
attach-less
among the illusory meaninglessness of things
where Self-Consciousness drifts, as to a cavern
and descends, and the sun narrowing and fading
and hollow sounds, and no sounds
and darkness, and free

that is not myself
or the No-Self, the *anatman*
not the lotus roots in the mud
the green pond, the tendrils and the carp
the floating leaves, the blossoms like cupped hands
whiter than the Himalayas
its white wind
cradling the Buddha

but orchards, rather, apples and pears
sweet sounds, sweet images
seducing me out of myself
a Consciousness no longer what it is
but what it sees and hears and touches
the fragrances and the blossoms
what Consciousness selects as real
—what least hurts in the mouth—
ah, delicious, this holiness
the apples and pears devouring me

The Mansion

elusive Self-Consciousness
mice scatter in the field when the scythe comes
rabbits dart to their burrows
oh, the heavy boots and the gun
foxes flee
and quail seek shelter in the deepest grass—
such is the quest for the mysterious

Self-Consciousness searching for its identity
the gothic mansion with its ghost, its phantom
the mystery in what garret, or gable
what closed door
what dungeon—
night-long with a lantern
the search for the ghost of nothing
the fearful and fragile light

till rest comes, and dreamless sleep
till dawn seeps through the dingy and damasked windows
and lo!
it wakes, bewildered by Being
nowhere and everything

When Unease Is Upon Me

when unease is upon me
I want to think continually of bliss
and sing my way to it
as if the sound of my own voice
were a salvation

although a box turtle in the field
as if gold mathematics made their way
blurred, slow, on a cumbersome carapace
crosses to somewhere

while above it
weedy as wild things are
ironweeds blossom, and asters, coneflowers and goldenrods
which need no intervention in the sun
no mantra, no incantations of deliverance

no one to say the unsayable
of what bliss is
not the box turtle, not the blossoms
not even the catbirds and chickadees
singing

Philosophical Substance

the *arhat*
his story of the boy who swims
a paradigm of the Self
the fish-boy and the boy-fish
river-fish and river-boy
all not the same, the same in endless change
thus change is substance

till the boy
amid his splashing strokes and tilting his head to breathe
stopped
and turning himself face-upward
floated, his breath feather-light
and was changeless

thus changelessness is substance
thus *nirvana* is *samsara, samsara* is *nirvana*
the paradox, each reality nestled in the other
utterly at rest
where minnows nibble at his ankles and wrists

Darwin at the Grand Canyon

Darwin, the cowboy
bringing from the bright world of the hemispheres
docked, that small ship
and biding his time among barnacles
did mount, finally, and brazened in a book
the mindlessness of what appears
mindful in the beaks of birds

and we are grateful
and yet, absurd and more absurd
is the everything beyond counting
without a trail down to the river
without the horse and horseman in the canyon
without Being, without the lightening flash
in which the slanted, reddened sun is merely light
merely vast

The Vacation

ah, paradox
which has a frown on its face—
why the golden bowl
why paradise
those images in the mind
the longed for

unlike the froth at the ocean's edge
the white, airy nothings fading in the sand
and froth again—
where is the Self
what damp footsteps when the eddies smooth the sand
those dear, small ripples of oblivion

and yet, who imagines paradise, or holiness
who observes the nothing—
not the gulls, the mist in the spray
the haze, or the blue beyond them
or the sun
when the paradox becomes
salt-scented, the Self
the dear dilemma

The Mourning Doves

when all is change
why the same sorrow
like the mourning doves
unless the various world is merely that
in essence, after all
repetitive as their honeyed moans
thus the urge to do, to make
out of creation's iterations
an admirably new song
has in its sound
an eternity of sameness

The Fountain

theologians have said of God
his plenitude is a fountain
ex nihilo
and then endless
unlike the stone horse
flexing in the plaza
in Lexington
spouting from its gaped mouth
a pretty and splashing stream
glittering, even
for the man not looking
or listening

The Dandelion Seeds

the minuscule of what is
the tiny seeds, each in an airy boll just off the ground
like nimbuses at dawn, in a green infinity
those tiny beings

on fibers thinner than the wisps of thought
or quarks, or bosons, or strings of the unseeable forever—
what point or purpose is there but to dream
where the tiny is preferable

anything is
even these words
to the sundering into the void without the white
pronged filaments

ah fragrant, the summer breeze as it embraces them
the caresses, the lofting of the Self
of Selves where death never quite is
although it is

The Frog

> *Old pond*
> *leap — splash*
> *a frog.*
>   Matsuo Basho 1686

what better, for phenomena
is the metaphor of the frog
the bullfrog, its bass *jug-a-rum* intermittent in the afternoon
as if to remind us

like the mud turtles, the water snakes
how we resemble, each to each
among the loosestrife, pickerel weed
pond lilies, cut grass

whatever the Other is
the tadpoles, the crayfish
the water striders, dragonflies, caddisflies
yet when it leaps, splash

from the bank
in its guise of whatever is
what does *leap* mean
what does *splash* mean

An Appalachian Song

> *Tears, idle tears, I know not what they mean*
> Alfred, Lord Tennyson

a divine despair
the poet said
unfocused, piercingly vague
though we know the stunted

the crow who is not the glory of god
who wrings from sorrow
as a banjo, a tenor in the mountains
never quite personal
more a weather of the inevitable
its harsh cries

not quite visible, that high voice
not the red-tail hawk or the screech owl
not quail or whippoorwill
or identified as to cause
or reason for its suffering

its vowels *e* and *a* and *i*
yet in flight
its despair is everywhere
on the landscape
inescapably beautiful

August

Self-Consciousness, but what is that?
the wind describing where its home is
or clouds their destination
the end of a raindrop
or where a leaf might fall, or an echo?

Self-Consciousness so vast we say *eternity, infinity*
the impossible to imagine
yet the loneliness somewhere under the ribs
seeks the nothingness of its beloved
its Buddha

ah, the sweet Self
there, in a lapse of Self-Consciousness, the thunderheads
the golden edge of the nimbus with impending rain
there, as the shower wanes, the light is everywhere
afterwards, singing

Walnuts

the fallen walnuts
a harvest greater than the squirrels' need
all that bounty in the yard and the yellowed leaves
the vivid green hulls
faintly nubbled, black-spotted

and raking them in the warm, waning sunlight
the pale blue and slight haze of the sky
the buckets-full for the trash
and as a way of assuring myself
that my pathos was not misplaced and sentimental
while raking them

not ignorant of Malthus and Darwin
and Egypt and Syria
those deaths and the refugees
and my dear aunt in hospice

but hapless, rather
an innocence, a mindfulness
an unforethought and guileless melancholy in the sun
artlessly suffering

Autumn

a yellow leaf
was all
touched my shoulder

The Hackberry Trees

without silence
without stillness
distress is on me
and I would blame it
bored with enlightenment
and with my aging body
on these Kentucky days
damp, chill and gray
till gazing at the hackberry trees outside my window
the trunks, the rough bark, serrated, silvery-dull
calms me
with the comfort of their Being
themselves
silent and still

The Protest

why would the universe
from the uninhabited, apparently
flame outward
and devolve to more and more complexity
defeating entropy by devouring its own existence
including ourselves
suddenly protest in the *Tao*

rejecting its maw
and in the *Analects*, in the *Lotus Sutra*
turn away, also, from the sensuous
from the man at the well who lifts the water for her
for a kiss

even the voice which explains its Being
it would mute
and make itself a mendicant robeless as a stone
and further, deny its Consciousness
emptied as husks of corn
as bean hulls

and for what
to know the meaninglessness of the stars
and close its lidded eyes, even, on those—
how death-like the holiness is

but for the smaller than a candle flame
the littlest seeds to sow
tinier than the sun in the east and west
is compassion
is the protest

The Wind Chimes

in my philosophy there are no kisses
no NASCAR, ESPN, no book clubs, neighborhood associations,
        church or hobbies
although old houses are endearing
the repairing of them, of mine
as if to receive a guest
as if preparing a nest, that old cliché
for what, it seems, I am incapable of

though I'm fond of books
and if the mind were sensual
caresses would be surcease enough
night long
for what the heart longs for
that other old cliché
that resonant metonymy
and letters, also
sometimes distraught, sometimes ranting

and a time or two in my philosophy
the sweet escape from the burden of the Self—
sometimes a phrase, a line
in the Immortality of Consciousness
sometimes a stanza is
eternal as a wind chime
ringing

Grackles

The Great Wave at Kanagawa (1829-1832)
Katsushika Hokusai

from the nothingness of light
as if chiseled from the whited, lilac clouds
the grackles come and idle in the sun-weary
weedy, empty lot
exclaiming for nothing in particular
with hushed cries, harsh, repeatedly

and the kids in the street are aimlessly at ease
languorous as cookies and milk
in an amnesty of play
until they torture the basketball to a stone
a sling

then they do not loaf any more
not the pretty girls, or the boys
the pale sweat on their foreheads, their damp hair
but are a childish petulance everywhere
their harsh cries, strident, repeatedly

and perhaps their shouts
startle the grackles to a swirling
a flutter of bodies as the children struggle
a curl of black flecks roiling
into nothingness

The Moon as a Prelude to Heaven

does it never end
the moon, I mean
pale even before sunset
the half-moon, waxing toward its glory
in autumn, immemorial

and who witnessed the moon
besides the poet and the names for it
Selene, Luna
and should it gather us up
in its pale luminance
anonymous as a shadow

a man, a woman
whose tides are miniscule in the blood
tugging the heart heavenward
in the invisible attraction beyond itself
beyond fleet Mercury, veiled Venus
the near dread and vengefulness of Mars

ah, zodiac of the stars
beyond which no meanings are but repetition
the circles, endlessness themselves
while we, torn from the moon
languish, love-lorn

The Sun

it gives us life, the sun
and the earth, too
and we are thankful for the light
and the seasoned earth, its bounty

yet we slaughter endlessly
and for the beautiful dying at our hands
we sing praises at the banquet—
and our own, oftentimes, we slay

the cross-uprighted and the pike
the knees-bent and scimitar
when every war is just
and familiar as the fingers curled in the palm

ah, paradox, the golden rays, the knife-thrusts of the sun
where the earth is a bowl for the sacrifice we pour and spill
lifting our hands, and the heart's blood of our praise
ecstatically

A Neon Moon

Brooks & Dunn

I wish, sometimes
when country music and its minor key
and whiskey, I have to admit
are an effort at making loneliness less boring
less tedious

to make it, instead, a purified effect
as the outdoors with its rose-pale, radiant maples
as the ginkos, more chartreuse than the sun
as it is now, the perfected song

I'll be alright
As long as there's light
From a neon moon

yet to be, rather, beyond that
serene as the hackberry trees outside my window
changeless in their galled leaves
all summer
and seared by the frost
their falling away in the cool, assuaging autumn
dull, and dingy yellow—
shabby, unkempt, to be in the leaf-fall
as Being

The Giggling Lama

long, long ago
there was a giggling lama
who, when questioned by the civil authorities
about the meaning of birth
said it's nothing
and giggled
and the same with questions about living
and suffering and dying
and the afterlife
they're nothing, he said, and giggled

the authorities were so angered they banished him
far away in the mountains
near the headwaters of the Mekong and the Yangtze
and the passersby
dreaming of the Pure Land, of Shambhala
heard in the wind the rippling snap of prayer flags
of the warriors' pennons
which were handclaps of the giggling lama

and among the rock falls and rushing streams
the sweeping mists and pale sun
were the gongs, the singing bowls, the prayer wheels—
the wind horses and the sky burial
ah, nothing will be nothing
not the griffon vultures
not the redstarts, or rose finches or ground jays
not the eared pheasants or the snow cocks of the temple
not even joy

The Hands

that western voice, Authority
as hands which would have, but for the desert
crumpled the *Gnostic Gospels*, the yellowed and flaking papyrus
into dust—and the murder of al-Hallaj
the Bogomils in a slaughter
Bruno at the stake
the Cathars murdered
the Quakers, the Ranters struck

till senility withered them as birds' claws
as carrion beaks
harvestless as skulls

and lo! bright Reason's hands
—fondling the Earth as if it were a foundling of the mind
an orphan doted on—
cast angels and myth and metaphor aside
as decorative joys and sorrows
and metaphysics also
until sweet Being, now
abides with its Self-Consciousness

swift as a goldfinch
glimpsed at
aware of nothing

The Stone Mason and the Monk

The Abbey of Gethsemani
The Sisters of Loretto

in what is called Kentucky's holy land
is a stone mason, a happy, laughing man who
when repairing the monastery wall before winter
let slip a stone
which struck him on the temple, and he fell
lying for a while unconscious—
awakening, he finished the stone work in half a day
without a memory of his labor
and when the monk, who dealt with restorations
approached
the mason, looking at the finished wall, smiled and laughed
yet the monk
among the rubble the man was clearing away
remembered reading
       in the palm
       how does grief fit
       like a pebble
and a few days afterward, on the monastery grounds
he meditated about four hours altogether—
awakening
he recalled, during that time, being Self-Conscious
but of nothing, of doing nothing in the emptiness
and he was at peace, his senses heightened, light-filled
yet, on his way back to the Abbey
among the oaks, poplars and hickories
he saw the happy, laughing mason
and was overwhelmed by a poem
       autumn leaves
       such a disguise
       for weeping

Another Love

>*amor intellectualis dei*
>Baruch Spinoza

estranged in October
in the first flurry of snow and fleet clouds
on a cold walk
how can it be that Enlightenment has occurred
(as noumena and the mind joined in an ecstasy)
and is now recognized by Self-Consciousness

when the *arhats* say that we, merely, are sensation
and that perception and ideas
some little permanence, like stones in a stream
are alien to the watery change of existence
which is the cause of *dukkha*, of suffering

yet we long to praise that source
to place lighted candles on the glittering stream
though our hands are clouds
and our praise as O-like as the harvest moon
voiceless as ripples on the water
where *nirvana* extinguishes all

ah, loneliness
the dear old man among his lenses and his axioms
anathematized
whispering that the mind is rarefied beyond clay
a gold of thought, gleaming in eternity

though I would choose, also, bound creature that I am
the imagination
causal as the bright leaves tumbling in reality
gamboge, cochineal

Winter

afternoon
the snow
and the blue shadows

The Snowstorm

such an odd word, *fractals*
used to calculate, amongst phenomena, branching
large to small, tree limbs to twigs
traced in the wintry mist
a grace of fine ice, and finer snow

until the branches
whiter than the whitened gray of the sky
fall, weighted down
plunging us into darkness
and cold

and men come
hoisted in the air on cranes
a rescue, rightening the wires and bringing comfort
the wafting of heat and light
to us

who are not indifferent to mathematics
or to the cold and dark
or the white mist and filigree, indifferent, we call beautiful
on the trees

The Poet Who Says Nothing

what news is there from somewhere other than myself
since all I am is a slathering of moods
as too many poets are
nutritionless as the wind

though the imagination can do wonders with a twig
the leaves fluttering god knows where
in a tiny, beautiful place
unfit for habitation

certainly not for Syrians, or Palestinians
not for the sexual rush in the bull
trampling the hyacinths in its path
or drones, passing like wasps over Yemen
or women raped in the Congo
or the dead in Bangladesh for the clothes we wear

perhaps if a mood were said just right
the phrase, the metaphor
ah, I've not heard that before, although I have
but never quite so expressed
it would be clever enough, outside myself enough
for listening to—
an idea resembling clouds
the birth of twilight
death and its eyeless tears

The Dog

a dog is chained next door
it has been since it was a pup
and I've noticed, on my several visits home, its growth
but the pathos now, however, is exceeded by its barking
its filthy body—
the rough square in the gray sheeting its house
the ten feet of its muddy hemisphere

if only the neighbors weren't so cruel
or that I, helpless
wouldn't wish its silence
or that al-Shabab on the evening news from Kenya
wasn't
or Typhoon Haiyan in the Philippines
wasn't
or that my sense of aesthetics, of meditation
truthful hypocrite
wasn't discredited

Ravi Shankar

at dawn
after my night
my laboring with words
is the stereo—
ah, ragas
the Brahman of the mind
his pulse in the tabla
his heart in the sweet, aching sorrowing of the sitar—
why can't my poems be
more than a listening—
why can't they be
but for the endless, dear, infinite grief
a Buddha
the desireless one
how can I sing
at dawn, of nothing

Heroes

why return from ecstasy
from the stilled eternity of empty light
why clamber down that old cliché
the great chain of being
and ask—embarrassed as a soul on stage, hiding its nakedness—
has compassion come from so obliterated a Self
from a Consciousness forgone, and, too, Self-Consciousness

how help, then, with meaningless hands, how loving-kindness
when the sun and all its flesh grow tall, and wider still
towering as an antlered elk, in bulk an elephant seal
a lion's mane, a tiger swift as blurred, colored winds
and the victims, each more wily than the next
more camouflaged, and swifter still
that are the offspring of our origin, the sun
devouring themselves so irresistibly that some men worship them
in an aristocracy of slaughter

except for the folk and their strange tales
a Hercules, a Beowulf, a Superman
whose contradiction stirs us, almost, to worship in the fantasy
in the daydreams of rescuing suns, our sons
our orphans of violent pity
so like, yet so unlike the vicious light of noon
and, too, the sweet birth of the weak, the dreamt of, also
the nimbus-ridden ones we've deified
the cross-strung and the self-denying one
who escape by fleeing the flesh they're born of
and want us, too, to flee where no sun is
but in the naked, suffering Consciousness which we
old-fashioned, call the soul

and though, in their bulked, erotic pity, our heroes dream of us
and our fleshless deities dream of caresses
their lidded eyes, the honeyed benedictions on the lips
          we long for—
the answer has its origin prior to
and before the sun, before the stars
before the heavens were
in the blazing darkness of pure nothingness
where the wanting of Pure Consciousness descends
and in Self-Conscious bliss, and suffering
it takes our hand, and smiles

Chicago

as a man from the countryside
and one who writes, though the word "poet" is pretentious
or so it seems to me
with its connotations of prophet and seer and divinely mad
none of which I am
but I do consider ideas about what and how we know
so, after a visit to Chicago, I wondered:
humanity so crowded, and separate from the soil
and why?

surely it's more than power
the absurd Sears tower and its X-ing up
or the Mercantile Exchange—
we have enough of that at home
in the chicken lot and the barn
and condescending comparisons won't do—
a hive, a queen brought brightness from the fields
or termites, or moles in their tunnels—
since it's humans, after all, on the trains
who joy and suffer as my neighbors do

yet words concern me
and William Carlos Williams comes to mind
no ideas but in things
(and I hope he didn't mean symbolist poetry)
but the point is
any thought of mine drifts in an ether of its own emptiness
        without a hayfield, without a moon
without a calf or hens

and what is the meaning of Chicago
a menorah, a Christmas wreath, trees wreathed in light—
it all seems artifice, a stone so polished it reflects the mind

arias and arabesques, semblances on the walls, and wailing blue
all transformed, as if, unbeknownst to itself
it were separate from the earth
and made—glorious city—an airy dearth
a deficiency beyond the soil
a dreaming, a metaphor

A Christmas Poem from an Atheist

pale gray, the sky
and pale white, the snow
so much one wishes for
not the high, branchy nest of squirrels
or the homeless cardinals
despite their wings
those we dream of in May
but not the slanted, perforated white air
of December
and why a born child
sweet Christmas child
in what is called the wind chill, the zero
without a blanket, a leaf cover
without its swaddling clothes
at least
for the sweet hope
of love

The Birdfeeder

the reality of the kitchen table
and the birdfeeder outside my window
what would they be
unobserved, unrecorded, without me
who includes them, inchoate things, in Being—
yet ridiculous is the repeated word, this *Being*
when the table, wordless
and the birdfeeder especially, filled with seed
as if waiting for the dawn
and sparrows
flitter-fussing and aggressive
to sing it
as if to chirp into existence
the sun

Meditation in December

where is the *there*
is it somewhere under the ribs
or in the braincase
or in the pale, harsh light when the days
such as this one
are at their worst

or is it the joy without paternity
the bathed birth and scented child
the murmured cooings of love in its inception
orphaned as the sky
or a joy without candied apricots and figs
without caresses, bodily, those fragments of ease

or a blossoming
stemless, petal-less, without fragrance
a rose and a not-rose
the slow foliation
the hammered foil and leafage about it
alone in bliss

Christmas Gifts

it doesn't matter
if we condescend to the hymns
and are superior to the gold foil on the myths
as iconoclasts—
the older ones, too, in the birth of the sun
Horus, Mithra, Sura, Tammuz

and yet they matter
the gift-seekers in the malls—
to see them as what they once were
as an infant, perhaps our child
matters
and we would give
which might be bought and wrapped
of love

yet with handless hands
reaching through the barren light
the meaning without meaning
lavishing on them thankfulness
who are the gift
naked as ourselves
in holiness, in bliss

The Christmas Moon

the moon
and all that's pagan and spring
shine unabashed this December 21st
almost a blasphemy
and Venus, too
in the night sky, its bright, slight blur

while Christmas lights, the modern LEDs
out-brave the dark
in the plethora of scattered rainbows
on porches and shrubs
and we, most un-Magi like
without gold, incense or myrrh, or gifts at all
set ourselves adrift
sentimental atheists on the streets
enjoying the miracle we don't believe in

while the moon and the evening star
glow in the solstice
indifferent to the cold
and to us
and to the paradox of love
the dear child soon to be
descending

The Necessity of Compassion

why is it light and ecstasy come at such cost
with its blank altogether
not the Christ kind, the Muhammad kind
the Reformation, the Inquisition
the Nazi, the Mao, the Khmer Rouge, the Taliban—
those are epiphanies and the death they bring

not a child's delight
the laughter which rings all sorrow from the world
with its sweet giggling
not lovers with their semblances of wings
the bird's cry and aerie of their bodies

all abandoned, nothing
where there is no birth, no life, no death
in the endless eternity of light
ah, no

surely something remains
in the nothingness of what we are
some care, some tenderness
of nothing

The Child

> *Out of the Cradle Endlessly Rocking*
> "The undertone—the savage old mother, incessantly
>   crying...."
>   Walt Whitman

when a child stumbles
and with a scraped knee
weeps
one doesn't accuse it of hypocrisy
and so with the Self
world-sobbing in its helplessness
one doesn't chide
as a dry philosopher
and warn against god-longing
and lecture on wrong reasoning
soteriology
but hugs and daubs and bandages
and briefly
like an old crone comforting in her withered arms
a child
sings of nothing and nothing and nothing

Winter and Spring

what the Self is
an enduring memory made anew
as if it were the same branches, the same twigs
ice-coated
and who would
as though distracted by a harsh light
the temperature at twenty degrees
look up

and against the cold-blue and blustery clouds of the sky
as if it were the same again
a half-century falling away
in the radiant, slender glittering of the twigs
neither boy nor old man
in the aesthetics of iced-over trees

the change and change again
the twigs that will bud in April, outward into leaf
the glittering and green in the same Self
the same phenomena of birth and death

and through them
as the glittering twigs clash in the wind
slivers of diamonds clinking as they fall
and April's bird calls in a sweet assist of leaves
assist the Self, and give it leave
into eternity

The Elk River

4-methylcyclohexanemethanol

the river
as if it were spooled paper
recording the spiked lines of a seismograph
the needle rippling like temblors
and near where the valleys merge
near the capitol and the golden dome
is the seeping rust of tanks
where multitudes are thirsting
waterless
there where the mountains rise
those beautiful boat-shapes of the sky
and higher and higher still
at the headwaters
is the trembling
where the stones are washed clean
far away
in the shattering of the mountains
among the clouds

Spring

March
the frogs cheep
and the heart, also

The Kentucky River Palisades

> *When the sun rises...I see the Heavenly host crying Holy Holy*
> *Holy is the Lord God Almighty*
>   William Blake

does it matter that the ecstasy is mine
alone, during the sweet loss of what I am
or that the twin of my experience, Self-Consciousness
rather than sublime
—a wedded ring of light, of the sun, chorusing—
is, rather, a white noise, hymn-less and void

like the hushed fluttering of bats at the Palisades
hurling twilight-wards, a darkness of identity
Self-Consciousness in which
equally without substance, are memory and desire
expressing the vague hum of eternity
but ah, the lack of that Consciousness and the sweet Self
the Self as a palisades

the cliffs with their wild rye, phlox, trillium and wild oats
their beech and yellow poplars, and higher up
the blue ash, rock elms, yellowwood, buckeyes, maples
a narrow sky and the high clouds, the cirrus at twilight
and at dawn, suffused, dove-gray and rose
in the mist, the sunrise

The Rainbow and the Raindrops

rather than utter the words
see the rainbow
one might say
now it is
or perhaps
it is now in its eternity

and what I have seen of rainbows
and also of drops of rain
—with some patience you can observe them
your shoulders dampened among low branches—
on the tips of leaves
dazzling little globes and scattered rainbows
before they swell and tremble and fall away

and my effort at describing them
an energy of the perpetual past tense
of yoking the metaphors to eternity
the rainbow, the raindrops
were

and the writing of them down
reviewing them in the mouth, on the tongue, the larynx
as if notations on a score, till they become
awkward as the expression is
pure vowels extended on the breath
as in *bliss* and *isness*

The Longing for Transcendence

the usher
it is his theater, too
and every waiter sees
linen, crystal, silverware
as well as those with hands at the napkin
the wineglass

and in the Civic Center
no one attends the trees
yet without them
bald as car horns
the streetlights would glower

and in the flat
the window looks to the moon
though not one pane is remarked on
ever
for its transparency

and as he nods off in his chair
tired as an elevator, a taxi
there's murmuring—
the angels, in a glory of halos
stand near his arm, weeping
            dream of us
            please dream of us

The Tea Roses

why not
in the capacious separateness of the mind
imagine the requital of our desire
only to find

in the consummation of our designs
at Giza, Agra, Chartres
the merely aesthetic
aching for eternity

or find in a rose
not a quaint symbol, heartfelt, of love
or what rose-ness is
but the fragrance of red, lingering
ringed, fragile and delicate, small to large

outward
till Consciousness, overwhelmed
in fear of fainting, merely, into petals
turns away
settling into nothing

Sweet Roses

> Let him be rich and weary, that at least,
> If goodness lead him not, yet weariness
> May toss him to my breast
> > George Herbert

we are caught up
as dust motes in the slants of light
the leafy shade, the ferns, the cliff, the cavern
and in the dreadful sun, also
all alien phenomena

so overwhelmed we dress them in metaphor
a masquerade, a grand hall
and dance
and the likeness lulls us
as an angel when an adjective

and Enlightenment
the wherewithal of ecstasy
when the joy of light
in a frenzy of stillness excluding us
and our symbols longing in their emulation
to make sweet roses where the stars are

fatigue us
as the lauded poet wrote, long ago
in a dear mistake
yet weariness may toss him to my breast
ah, not quite that
—how love what longs to love?—
unless it be
serene, desireless as eternity

The Guitar

The Man with the Blue Guitar
Wallace Stevens

if life forms are a devouring out of the sun
when the time comes, disillusioned
what would the mind, that little sun
devour

does it feast on rhetoric, on metaphor
eating its way to nothingness
and suspire in the glory of its unbecoming
drained of its ecstasy

or rather, in the complexity of stars
from whose eddying we are
when a star, no longer quite itself
sustains a planet

the mind says, ah, blue as a guitar
the man who plucks it, and strums
a beloved pretense, an aesthetics
not himself but rapt in a simulacrum

The Seasons

> "Annihilating all that's made
> to a green thought in a green shade."
> *The Garden*
>
> Andrew Marvell

a summer's loss
ah, what a great cost is Buddha
having to forgo, as tumbling leaves
ourselves stem-torn from the twigs
branches and limbs
and become
vivid flickers of wind—
and the mind-held
to forgo that, too
not even leaf mold, flecked-brown, underfoot
bare as winter
all forgone—
not even spring
when semblances, blossom-shaped, of saffron
of banners and pennants scattered on the ground
bluets, henbit, chickweed, white clover, spring beauties
the earth seems
in our simplest hearts, to sing of everything

Winged Horses and the Alphabet

why write about suffering as it rises in the mind
our inevitable death, that subject
and think that a reader would be interested and sympathetic
unless I could, intriguingly, present it—an iTune, a
        YouTube—an *Om* disguised as I and you where nothing
        was before a voice which

oddly enough
hums reality as existent things to see and speak of in a breath
engaging enough as a Tweet
then I might suggest

that I am reality, though it's you of course
and without me, the you and I
phenomena would not be different
but merely voiceless as the stones are, and the clouds

we have dreamed reality as existent
a fantasy with an origin in the vowel *o*
in the consonant *l* and others of their kind
and we have made ourselves ethereal figures

fictions awakening to the fact of death
to a Self-Consciousness which is
after all our suffering, merely
intangible as a breath

The Tulip Magnolias

woody orchids, lily magnolias, red magnolias
purple magnolias, saucer magnolias

ah April
half my life I pursued what joy means
and now, in retrospect, as if knowing all along
in that moment of ecstasy, long ago, my nothingness
there was April and its tulip magnolias

their blossoms should be near the ground
like hollyhocks and gladiolus, not flowering high up
gaudy and flaunting themselves on leafless limbs
bare as the month is when the equinox arrives
touching as it does the twigged green meaning of reality

the sepals themselves bizarre
brown, thumb-sized, velvety, shriveling and falling away
and the blossoms
the inner side pale white, the outer pink and mauve
which, I'm fairly sure
do not speak of something other than themselves

nor do I
bored and distressed a little by their repetition
create fallacies of them—ah, two-colored petals
so like the mind in its diversity
the crooked twigs and the leaves—

and as felt thought, more than an image
see shapes and hues uncountable
as palms upturned for an unintentional gift—
no, just idly observant, not really Buddhist
not mindful in the nothingness of joy
absurd and holy and glorious

Butterflies, Moths and Birds

the pronoun *I*
who can explain it
among the foliage and heat of the day
like a butterfly, stumbling from its chrysalis
pausing for its spread wings to dry

and as the one great miracle of humanity
no longer earth-bound but fluttering
in a synesthesia of sound
syllables against the green and blue of what
today, we call phenomena

ah, the parti-colored grammar
gold and black, brown and silvery gray
and the green glory of the luna moth—
and the mouths of birds, also
the trills and calls
their syntax hidden among the trees

sentences for the person as a separate Self
fluttering and trilling
with its lonely cry for what
in a bit of sound
is called love with its liege companion
ah its sweet language

The Abandoned Field

until the fresh leaves and the rainfall
I had Reason to cling to—
all else was discarded
Deity Soul Mind
mere words, illusory metaphysics

as was the *Noumena*, the trans-phenomenal
stilled, their void a rescue from impermanence
since how could nothing change
pure, distant, untouchable
without birth or life or death
until the poplar leaves

broad and large on a sapling
like gangly adolescents, boys and girls
trembled in the scented spring and the rain
unaware of the wherefore of their shuddering
as I was of my desire for union

until the rivulet at the edge of the field
the stones there, unaware of the gurgling of April
of my heart's distress until, dear freedom
the gain of that idea in metaphysics—
Time and Eternity are one
Phenomena and Noumena are one
Samsara and Nirvana are one

The Killdeer

who would have thought
given my condition at seventy-five
what with my misery in the parking lot
that a small bird could lift my burden away
the killdeer that lighted on the curb
and strolled, delicately long-legged
like a slender girl on a four-inch promenade
between the asphalt and the grass
nodding her head as if to a beau
as if to show her double breast-band for him
a simple loveliness, black and white
demure as she dawdled
like Jenny with the light-brown hair

and the other tribulation
fraught as it was with panic
the gasp and caught breath, when every third thought
when, imagining death, one races on a mapless map away
but the killdeer was much too elegant to be the metaphor
        of what I sorrowed for
too graceful, too comely for a sobbing, sentimental end
ubiquitous as it is, commonplace as the dying and
        their farewells
but it was mine, my sorrow, that the shapely creature
indifferent in its charm, helped lift away

and a paramour, as surprises are
in a flash of white breast and orange-brown rump
was of a sudden there, and politely strutting for a while
leaped atop her and tread, almost daintily
and presumably the little ruffle and shudder was sex
after which he leaped down, swaggered and bobbed a bit
and was off

and my labor, after all that study of a moment's light
the implications of its delight, as mystical, as Being
is pointless now because eternity, wrapped in phenomena
is an inference from that ecstasy, and in any case, a logic lost
every reason gone
when the mind imagines its own oblivion while she—
serene, minus a crown, carriage or a retinue
nonchalant as a queen—stepped to her green paradise
　　　　and feasted on—
too refined to see—what insect it was, or seed

The Tulips

of what use is ecstasy
which now, Self-Consciousness as a judge
is deemed a yesterday
not of a giggling joy but a threshold to suffering
a mansion, an estate-sale emptied, even, of itself
which does not yield the quotient of anything
in the tally of phenomena
or issue into Being as the walls come down
an imperium of airy forms, or pierceless palms
or a mawless arbor of quietude

Self-Consciousness, nightlong
is a dance, a metaphor of gold and glittering
a refulgence without light, an imitation sun, a searching
and yet what use is that
when Enlightenment sorrows us beyond weeping
beyond the temple or cross or minaret
or doom or fate
in the infinite, bright meaninglessness of *now*
of Being

here, in the time-bound night of April
in the warm, moist darkling of my yard, tulips have risen
and in the metaphysics of the inseparable
their petals are the surcease, in their helpless beauty
of estrangement, of *samsara* and *nirvana*
and as a philosophy
each Enlightenment is a handmaiden to a flower
as compassion is, brother and sister
to the light without light
of nothing

Enlightenment

that Enlightenment
that everywhere which might
or not, illuminate whomever
whether the mind is a No-Self
indiscriminate, memoryless as the wind
or as the sun or moon
Enlightenment illuminates whatever nonetheless

and yet, what matters that
or clearing brush away
weeds from the garden plot
sense after sense—wild roses by the creek
fox grapes from the electric poles
and memory, also, and thought
burning the debris till Consciousness
in its purity, is a countless identity of itself

whether I pour into its Being
or not, my heart—whether I praise or not
or linger with the longest vowels
and the pulse of tympanis
in an aria of what I long for
ah, guiltless love,
some eternal Beingness of desire

whether roses or not
in the paradise of June, flawed endlessly
of fragrant trellises, of creamy and scarlet blooms
or honeysuckle, scented nightlong along the fence
whether ontology or not
or existent or substance
its refulgence *is* and *now*
eternally

The Ark

what is left
after the deconstruction
after Schopenhauer and Nietzsche
Heidegger and Wittgenstein
Derrida and Foucault
when *Self* merely points to an animal
when *Consciousness* is nothing more than intent
when *Self-Consciousness* is an aftereffect of language
when *Pure Consciousness* is ineffable—

what is left
after enlightenment
after Hume and Kant
after Shankara and Ramanuja
after the meaningless meaning of whatever ultimately is
its sweet bliss
its fading afterimage of eternity—
what is the pronoun *I* or *myself* or *me*
what is the meaning of my name
or yours, or any name

that ontology of Being
that transparent intelligence
blue at the furtherest reach, like the sky
and an ark, nearby
anticipating reality all spring
two by two

The Metaphors of Phenomena

if we were as raindrops are
we would sculpt fountains by the sea
as fiery as the sun
we would forge bronzes of flambeaus
as the winds are
we would cast chimes to capture them
as leaves are
we would stretch canopies of silk
as stones are
we would raise temples to the clouds
as evanescent dew
we would sing sweet sorrows to the sky
as endless death
we would imagine dances, endlessly

The Weeds

without imagery but for a walk among weeds
—yarrow, asters, boneset, wild carrot—
and their nothingness is everywhere in phenomena
which, however glorious
have no more substance than the moments they exist in
a mindless and mystic *now*

and they would
if we were childish in our minds, merely Conscious
suffice
and would be fabulous there
a delight of causes and their odd effects
— horses with wings and lambs and lions of the gods—

but not at present
not in Self-Consciousness
where phenomena are a blank bedecked with every loss
a nihilism of ironweed, sow thistles, joe-pie weeds
cobwebbing with their presence all that is not
that terror of the Self, a causeless nothing
the anathema, lonely, breathless
without sanity or a sigh of love

but that, too, is a childishness
though a superior kind
and is overcome
when the Self turns, as it will, to Self-Conscious reason
there, where causes aren't willy-nilly
—desire's imagining and a chaos of effects
delirious angel-clouds and stones with eyes—

but sober, dull, boring
loosed of all absolutes but inferences of causation
and Self-Consciousness understands, soon enough
contingent as causes are

and infinite in their reach
that they recede and stretch forth
forever

and so, unintentionally
in the contemplation of their unity
Self-Consciousness becomes Pure Consciousness
there where the milkweed and mullein
pokeweed, ironweed, boneset and asters
all in the weed-flanked, crowded path
are holiness, are Being

The Wedding

it's time to celebrate!
the world will devour itself, sure enough
children will giggle in their paradise
lovers will praise, in halves
the brief ecstasy they have
in hyperboles of drying seas

but ah, this is the season, in leafing out
when it cavorts and shouts
chaste as chlorophyll
as steers' eyes, as slender deer
moon-eyed, and bees, blossom-wards
and the birds waking and warbling
and the silvery glittering on the leaves

and the observer of them
the ball cap—the mind, Self-Consciousness—
all finished but for the laughter
the wedding vows
and petals of flowers
and all dear thoughts are unlearned
since like the golden bee, and nectar
they, too, are eternity

Postscript: History and Fate

As defined in commentaries on mysticism, what I experienced in 1968 was enlightenment, as pompous as that sounds, and it happened so many years ago—and was so seldom repeated—that it now seems like a fairy tale. Once upon a time, long ago, a man became, not himself but an eternity of light, and lo.... Since I am writing this postscript in 2014, forty-six years is not that long ago, not an era, although "the sixties" might be appropriate for initiating the second half of the 20th Century.

Historical conjunctions (as another name for fate) are significant in this brief essay on Buddhism and my rejection of its fundamental tenets. The majority of Americans were experiencing the post-war liberalism of the fifties and sixties—the Warren Court, the Civil Rights movement, the increasing wealth of the middle class, and the cultural revolution culminating in the early seventies, important not only for the anti-war protests but also for the increased interest in Asian religion.

Meanwhile, nearly as far away from those cultural events as possible, my experiences in the forties and fifties were the coal camps and pentecostal churches of southern West Virginia, from which I escaped by joining the Navy in 1956. In my case, the blind indifference of fate cast me ashore for two years of duty in Japan where, as a late-developing teenager, I responded to the austere beauty of Buddhism with an awestruck reverence befitting my abysmal ignorance.

The same fate brought me closer to a blending with America at large by tossing my father, a career Army sergeant, into the Presidio in San Francisco, where he married a cashier at the PX, and then, when he retired, settled in the city. So I made my way to the world of beatniks and City Lights, to San Francisco State and Haight Street and the hippies. There, between tokes, I read several books on the subject of mysticism.

The convergence was nearly complete by 1968. I had an M.A. in English from San Francisco State, a backpack of commentaries on mysticism, a kilo of marijuana, and with what seemed like a long, intermittent nightmare, the deaths of Martin Luther

King, Jr. and Robert Kennedy. That summer, after snagging a teaching job in eastern Kentucky, I wandered the wilds of strip-mined Boone County, West Virginia, stoned and primed for an enlightened experience, which did happen, and so did, soon afterwards, a mental crisis with which I entered the adult world at the age of thirty.

There was a cultural fusion on that dirt road as well. My insignificant self was saturated with the cultural ideas of the previous century, the romantic idealism of Wordsworth and Whitman in their search for transcendental meaning, so I interpreted my enlightened experience as a beatific union of myself and the spiritual essence of reality. I was a dancing fool, a holy fool on a dirt road; yet myself as a minor collation of 19th Century culture—its beatific ideal—met its opposite in malefic materialism, in my case experiencing the lush vegetation along the very same dirt road as alien, hostile presences loosed on the world by Darwin and Wallace. The irony was that I taught college freshmen about cultural currents which had shattered my psyche.

Southern West Virginia and eastern Kentucky were some distance from the contemporary cultural events of America in the early seventies, an aerie of mountains away from chaos, so the connection faded until my Ph.D. studies at Ohio University where, with the Kent State killings, my memories of the riots at San Francisco State and Berkley came to life with the tear gas and police on campus. Indifferent fate had intruded on what I thought was a personal choice of a university, and so there was a yoking once again of my individual self and an era-defining event in America. What chance was there for happiness, for serenity and peace, when I had no control over cultural events and none over fate?

If I were truly middle-class and a product of the secular humanism then current in the universities, I could have considered my enlightenment the way one does an oceanic experience, an epiphany in the shower, for example, or blissfulness on the swing-set, but a pentecostal upbringing includes a revelatory ecstasy, a transcendence of wickedness and sorrow through personal salvation and an end-times eschatology. It also includes the excruciating boredom and the horror of punishment during the interminable repetition of the words *Christ, Hell* and *Salvation*. Tossing all that aside except for the need of ecstasy, I was preparing myself for spiritual understanding by finding another path toward it. I began to read on the subject. The trajectory of my reading was always parallel to my enlightened experience in 1968, and I came to the conclusion that, since the experience was ineffable, nothing could be said about it except for the psychological responses of ecstasy and an intense sensation of light. *Any meaning attached to the enlightened experience is spurious.* Oddly enough, and a pathos of logic, is that I did not ask myself if enlightenment were actually an experience with a trans-phenomenal reality or if it were merely self-referential.

In a human context, forty-six years is quite an expanse of time, and no one could spend it in meditation, especially if one marries, becomes a parent, divorces, has a few affairs with both men and women, and betwixt times grades forty years of freshman comp papers. However, since my mystical reading kept pointing to the phenomenal world as somehow unreal—*maya, samsara*—I decided to investigate that world by reading in the sciences, layman's reading because I don't understand mathematical equations. And good god, no wonder the thinking man and woman would look for meaning in something other than the material world, since it is in a constant state of change, and low-entopic systems, the plants and animals, require a constant devouring of themselves for their existence.

Fate, of course, had to toss me to the far west of Tennessee, the land of soybeans, milo, corn and winter wheat, thirty miles from the Mississippi River, hours from Saint Louis, Memphis and Nashville, but the isolation might have been good fortune, though certainly in disguise, because while there, rather than drink and dope myself to death, I raised a child, published four books and created eight others in manuscript form. Not satisfied with my reading in the sciences, I turned to philosophy, and though my reading was frequently not in the original and often slapdash, I discovered, like Buddha, that most all metaphysics could be tossed out the window, except perhaps for Nagarjuna, Shankara, Hume and Kant, especially Kant's *noumenon*, which I associated with the ineffable reality experienced during enlightenment, particularly if accompanied by ecstasy so intense that light, physiologically and psychologically, became a symbol for it.

With all that reading, and with an occasional flash of what happened to me all those years ago, appropriately enough alongside a creek at the Land Between the Lakes, a convergence of Western culture and my mystical view occurred. The postmodern world—that of Schopenhauer, Nietzsche, Heidegger, Wittgenstein, Derrida and Foucault—was just a step away from the meaningless meaning of the enlightened experience. Without that experience, or so it seems to me, one accepts the self-defeating irony and the nihilism current in our Western capitalist culture. I refused to accept Western deconstructionism and rampant capitalism as the basis of my spiritual point of view.

To my satisfaction at least, there was a merging, not only of my personal life and cultural events in America, especially with my initiating Blair Mountain Press, but also a convergence of Western and Eastern philosophy in my synthesis of deconstructionism and the meaningless meaning of the enlightened experience. And yet fate has a way of confounding the happiest of circumstances, although I was a contributor this time to my own distress. As a retired person, I wanted to keep my mind as active as possible, so I started a new round of mystical reading and a new round of poems, *Letters to Buddha*, of which this postscript is a part. In an earlier book, *Twofold Consciousness: Poems and Essays on Mysticism*, I expressed some skepticism about the Buddhist concepts of *samsara* (the phenomenal world), *annata* (the no-self), and *nirvana* (liberation from *samsara*).

Frankly, whatever my enlightened experience may have been, or whatever little wisdom I may have gained through my studies, they did not prepare me for the death anxiety I began to suffer at age seventy-five, so much so that I questioned once again the trans-phenomenal reality which is revealed during enlightenment. Even though enlightenment has no content relevant to human affairs—and in that regard is meaningless—it was still a noumenal reality, eternal and light-filled, in which phenomena, including myself, participated, and thus provided an immortality which the Buddhists call *nirvana*. From that point of view, nirvana is soteriological. It is salvation.

In the poems, I emphasized the self and phenomena as ontological realities, whereas self-consciousness and our language world are contingent realities, so much so as to be epiphenomenal. So, unless the Buddhist concept of *annata*—a no-self—referred to self-consciousness, and unless *samsara* (the phenomenal world) and *nirvana* (noumenal reality expressed as phenomena) are one, then I would have to reject those concepts. I had never accepted reincarnation and its concomitant *karma*, since those concepts are clearly transcendental, but I did think that the Four Noble Truths and the Noble Eightfold Path were profound pronouncements on life. However, if the basic reality of life is desire, which is the cause of all suffering, and if to end suffering is to end desire, the ultimate of which is enlightenment, then the enlightened experience is being used in the service of a concept, a metaphysics, I don't agree with.

It is a metaphysics based on the idea that the unsatisfactoriness of life is the cause of suffering, that the self is not a consistent entity but a creature of continual change among phenomena, and that a release from suffering and change is achieved through an experience of enlightenment, which is a liberation from phenomena, an extinguishment altogether of the continually changing entity called the self.

There is no meaning to the enlightened experience but what is self-consciously attached to it afterwards. For me, the afterwards is an absolute blank but for the remembrance of light and ecstasy. Even my concept of meaningless meaning requires a very self-conscious metaphysics, which is rationally cogent but ultimately irrelevant to the ineffable experience. The only active expression of enlightenment is, for me personally, figurative language, poetry, which approximates reality but never is, or claims to be, reality itself.

How unfortunate—and there's fate again (or cosmic irony)—that light, ecstasy and eternity require the meditative state of pure consciousness for the perception of them because pure consciousness depends on self-consciousness; self-consciousness requires a self and its intentional states; and the self requires a material world in which to function. Self-consciousness, that glory of our intelligent species, retains the memory of enlightenment, yet it is also knowledgeable of its own annihilation. That's fate, our mystic reality with its joyful illumination in contrast to existential reality with its meaningless meaning of enlightenment and the fact of death. However, my philosophy of meaningless meaning is imbued with suffering and, arising from it, a sympathy for life, a loving-kindness and compassion for existence. Kant spoke of Practical Reason, of an *a priori*, innate moral sense, which I believe we have, independent of God or the enlightened experience. Enlightenment reveals to us our helplessness, our human condition, and thus is an impetus to compassion.

That philosophy with its existential responsibility of compassion should be enough to sustain an adult, yet almost half of the poems in *Letters to Buddha*—twenty-eight of them—are syntactically not of the declarative but the interrogative, as if a child were asking, how come my chest hurts?, as though there were an answer as to why we have a spiritual longing with a requital of meaninglessness.   Our helplessness when confronted by phenomenal reality, by death and suffering, is so overwhelming that we (or I) cry out beyond the assurance of existential compassion and practical reason for a rescue from it; and yet the enlightened experience of ecstasy and light merely *is*. It has no more rational or sotereological content than a budding leaf or a falling one. Noumenal reality, the self, and phenomenal reality are one; *samsara* and *nirvana* are one. And so we suffer and long for rescue. From my perspective, some comfort comes from the belief that noumenal reality is an actuality, an existent, a substance, an ontology, what in the poems I call Being and holiness. I have no way of justifying my belief except to say that it is a comfort to me and a reason for universal sympathy.

There's no escape from the fact of dying, and since I am much nearer to it than far, when I completed the book I collapsed for a while into fear and panic, and a recovery still not complete. I would prefer that the pentecostal dream not be so difficult to put aside and that the Buddha dream not so difficult to conceptualize, since there are real differences between Mahayana and Hinayana Buddhism. It would be a great comfort to believe in a transphenomenal reality which would sustain the self somehow beyond its annihilation, but that belief depends on self-consciousness, which is mortal. Ah. Who will comfort me as I lie dying? Would it be Whitman's fierce old mother? Would it be Stevens' death, who is the mother of beauty? Or rescue through an aesthetic realm in the immortality of consciousness? Or rescue by merging with the defining currents of culture? Or the mindless urgency of the universe, the noumenon of reality which will come, soon enough, to be my immortality? Perhaps so, although I hope it will be my daughter, at the finish, who will hold my hand.